...IF YOU LIVED AT THE TIME OF THE
Great San Francisco Earthquake

by ELLEN LEVINE

illustrated by RICHARD WILLIAMS

SCHOLASTIC INC.

New York Toronto London Auckland Sydney

*To Nathan, Ide, and Mac; and Carol, for finding
the refugee shacks at midnight.*

*Special thanks for their invaluable help to
Eva Moore, my editor;
Gladys Hansen, San Francisco Archivist;
and Jane Cryan, founder of the Society
for the Preservation & Appreciation of
San Francisco's Refugee Shacks.*

ISBN 0-590-40372-9

Copyright © 1987 by Ellen Levine.
Illustrations copyright © 1987 by Scholastic Books, Inc.
All rights reserved. Published by Scholastic Inc.
Art direction by Diana Hrisinko.
Text design by Emmeline Hsi.

12 11 10 9 8 7 6 5 4 3   8 9/8 0 1 2/9
                                                              08
Printed in the U.S.A.
First Scholastic printing, April 1987

CONTENTS

Introduction

In 1906, San Francisco was the biggest city on the West Coast. Nearly half a million people lived there. Most people lived in wooden houses and took trolley cars or cable cars to go to work or to school.

Very few people had automobiles, and nobody had radios or television sets — they weren't invented yet. Most people learned what was happening in the city and in other places by reading newspapers.

Then, on Wednesday, April 18, 1906, a terrible disaster struck San Francisco. A little after five o'clock in the morning, a huge earthquake hit the city.

The earth twisted, rumbled, and shook for nearly fifty seconds. If that seems like a short time to you, try jumping up and down for fifty seconds. You'll see that it feels much longer than it sounds.

Inside houses, pictures fell off the walls, lamps crashed to the floor, furniture raced around the room, books flew through the air, mirrors cracked into tiny pieces, walls caved in, and people were thrown from one end of a room to the other.

Three hours later, at eight o'clock in the morning, a second big quake hit the city. Then the earthquake was finally over. But the worst was still to come. For three days and nights, fires burned the city. The fires were so bright that you could read a newspaper at midnight. When it was over, there was little left of San Francisco. The city lay in ashes.

This book tells what it was like to live through all the shaking, rumbling, and burning of one of the biggest earthquakes the United States has ever known.

What did San Francisco look like after the earthquake?

Everything was a mess! There were cracks in the streets that looked like giant zigzags. If you stood in one, it might be as high as your waist.

Telephone and electric wires had snapped and were hanging down from the poles. Cable car tracks that were in the ground were suddenly sticking up like huge, bent paper clips. And trolley car tracks lay twisted in the street.

Some trees had been pulled up by the roots. Branches were cracked and scattered around.

Chimneys had broken off rooftops throughout the city. Some chimneys had fallen inside homes, others were lying in the streets. In parts of the city, whole buildings had collapsed.

Walls of the new city hall building had fallen down. The dome was left standing on top of steel pillars. It had been the largest building in the state of California. After the earthquake, it looked like a skeleton.

The front wall of one hotel fell off completely, and the bedrooms looked like rooms in a doll's house. Can you imagine sitting in your bed and looking out at the street — with no windows in between!

Some buildings that were three or four stories high sank almost all the way into cracks in the ground. One nine-year-old girl remembered that her father took her out of their house through the attic window right onto the street.

Houses moved forward, backward, or sideways. If you went to bed on April 17th on one side of the street, you might have gotten up on April 18th across the street.

After the quake, one man climbed to the top of a hill and looked down on the city. From up high, people in the streets looked as if they were "running about like . . . excited insects."

Throughout San Francisco, water pipes had been broken by the earthquake. In some places, water was spurting up from the ground.

A cloud of dust filled the air. At times it was as thick as fog, and you couldn't see your hand in front of you. As the fires spread, there was smoke everywhere. It made your throat feel scratchy and your eyes itch.

Saddest of all was the sight of wounded or dead people and animals lying in the streets.

Who was up at the time of the quake?

Not many people. Almost everyone was asleep. But if you think about what happens early in the morning, you can probably figure out who was up when the earthquake hit.

All the people who worked in the vege-table and fruit markets were already on the

job. The sidewalks were piled high with bags of onions, potatoes, carrots, and other vegetables.

The butchers and fish sellers had been working since four o'clock in the morning. They were loading food onto trucks to deliver to stores for the morning shoppers.

A few trolley cars and cable cars were running. The early morning workers were going to their jobs. The people who worked very late were riding home.

The milk carriers were already delivering the milk cans, and some newspaper reporters had just finished writing their stories from the night before. They were heading home.

Throughout the city, walking up and down the streets, were the police officers on duty at that early hour.

There were other people, too, who were up — because they couldn't fall asleep.

What did people do when the quake struck?

It was a little after five o'clock in the morning when the earthquake struck, and most people were asleep. It was a frightening way to wake up. Many people were so stunned that they ran straight out into the streets.

When they got outside, they realized that they were in their pajamas and nightgowns! Some didn't care and just stayed outside until the earth stopped shaking. Many people didn't take the time to put on shoes, and that was dangerous — there was broken glass all over the ground.

One man was seen running down the street with his pants on backward, his suspenders hanging down the front, and his shoes unlaced.

Another man was wearing his top hat and his fancy evening tailcoat. Underneath the coat, all he had on was his long underwear!

These people may have looked silly, but they were lucky to be alive and outside.

A man named David Frazier was sleeping in a folding bed. When the earthquake hit, the bed snapped closed and he was trapped inside, bent over like a jackknife. He could hardly breathe, and was rescued just in time by a police officer who helped him to safety.

How many people died?

We don't know exactly how many people were killed. At the time of the earthquake, city officials believed that nearly 500 people had died.

But since then we have learned new information. Gladys Hansen is the archivist (ARE-ki-vist) for San Francisco. That means that it is her job to know about the history of the city and its government.

Ms. Hansen believes that many more than 500 people died in the earthquake. She has worked like a detective in search of the *real* story about what happened.

BULLET

WANTED!

NAME OF ANY PERSON WHO LIVED IN OR WAS VISITING SAN FRANCISCO IN APRIL, 1906

THANK YOU FOR YOUR HELP!

First, she read all the old newspapers from 1906, and any magazines and official city books. She began to keep her own list of all the names of people who had died.

Then she sent letters to newspapers, magazines, and clubs all over the country. She asked if anyone knew about someone who had been in San Francisco at the time of the quake.

She received hundreds of letters filled with stories about the 1906 disaster. Her list of the dead now has more than 2,000 names, and the letters are still coming in! The 1906 quake is an old story, but we don't yet know the final ending.

What did the earthquake sound like?

A group of scientists talked with many people who had lived through the quake. They asked them what it had sounded like. Almost everyone said there was a great rumbling and a roaring.

But there were other answers as well. These are the very words people used to describe what the quake sounded like to them:

— a stampede of cattle
— a heavy hailstorm
— thunder underground
— strong wind in the trees
— a locomotive coming at full speed
— a loud clap
— wagons crossing a bridge
— a string of firecrackers

If you read the list slowly again and try to hear the sounds in your mind, you will

know what it was like to be in the middle of San Francisco in 1906.

What did the earthquake look like?

People who were up at the time and out on the streets actually saw the earthquake as it was happening.

Police Sergeant Jesse Cook was on duty in the vegetable market. As he looked up, he saw the street splitting open in front of his eyes. In one place, it opened six feet and then closed up again.

Buildings swayed and shook. One man said they looked as if they were dancing.

Frank Ames was a newspaper reporter who had worked until the early morning hours. He saw all the cobblestones in the streets jumping up and down. He said they looked as if they were alive!

Some people saw trees bend over with their tops touching the ground. And one man watched a heavy wagon move five feet forward and then back and then forward again at least three times.

Everybody said the ground rolled like waves on the ocean. Try to imagine that. It means that anything in the path of the earthquake would rise up and then fall down — telephone poles, stores, houses, wagons, streetlights, trees, cars, restaurants, and even people!

What did the earthquake feel like?

Most people woke up at 5:12 in the morning because their beds were bumping and sliding around their rooms. It was some way to start the day!

Frank Ames said he felt as if he was in an elevator going down fast, sinking.

Anna Amelia Holshouser said she "danced" all the time she was trying to get dressed. Her legs kept bending and straightening, and she found herself jumping up and falling all around the room.

Colonel Mullally said it felt as if two invisible giants were wrestling under the hotel where he was staying.

One woman's house moved four feet down the road and then bumped along the ground for a while. She said she felt "like corn in a popper."

Have you ever been in an earthquake? What did it feel like to you?

How big was the earthquake?

Scientists know how to measure the strength of earthquakes. They use what they call the Richter (RIK-ter) scale. The scale is a list of numbers that goes from one to nine. An earthquake that measures over six usually causes a great deal of harm. The 1906 San Francisco earthquake at 5:12 A.M. measured more than eight!

There are millions of earthquakes every year, but most of them are too small to feel. In the great San Francisco quake, you could feel the earth shaking from Los Angeles, California, to Coos Bay, Oregon — about 730 miles. It would take you about a day and a half to drive that whole distance.

The earthquake split the ground open for hundreds of miles. From up above, the crack looked like a crooked line. In some places, the ground on either side of the line moved twenty feet apart.

Imagine that your house was sitting right on the earthquake line. You and your sister or brother shared a bedroom with your beds side-by-side. After the earthquake, the two of you might be in two different rooms! And one of you might even be four feet higher up than the other. That's because the ground not only moved back and forth, but also up and down.

It's not surprising that some people called this earthquake "The Great Shake!"

Were there any warnings that an earthquake was coming?

At five o'clock in the morning on April 18th, nobody knew that the earth was going to rise and sink and crack open just a few minutes later.

In fact, the night before the quake, it seemed that all of San Francisco was celebrating. The famous singer, Enrico Caruso, was singing at the opera house. And there was a big roller skating party at the arena called Mechanics Pavilion.

But looking back and remembering what happened just before the quake, some people believe there *were* warnings.

The night before, horses whinnied, snorted, and beat their hooves against the stable stalls. Cows outside the city were restless. Some stampeded. Dogs howled through the night and into the early morning hours.

One person reported that her dog ran around the house for ten seconds before the earthquake. Then it jumped out an open window one floor above the ground. It seemed the animals knew something frightening was about to happen.

There were even some warnings for people, but nobody knew what they meant.

Mr. McConnell had a jewelry store in San Francisco. Four days before the earthquake,

one store window had broken into fifty pieces, but none had fallen out. At first he thought a burglar had tried to get in. But the police captain investigated and said, "No." The whole building had moved slightly — just enough to break a window!

We don't always notice signs or warnings. And even if we do, often we don't know what they mean.

How did animals act when the quake hit?

In some ways, they acted like people. Horses screamed, dogs and cats cried, and many animals shivered in terror.

Cats rushed around wildly with their tails all puffed out, and some carried off their kittens to hiding places. Dogs ran off, and some didn't return for days. Others stayed close to people for many hours.

One mule refused to eat all day.

Outside the city, cows came down from grazing in the hills and wouldn't go back up for days. And they wouldn't give milk, either.

Some cows gave birth before they were supposed to, and we know of at least two cows that died from shock.

There were about 200 circus animals in San Francisco at the time of the earthquake. Most of them crouched down close to the ground while it was happening. When it was over, the elephant raised its trunk high in the air and roared. All the other animals followed its lead. We'll never know if they were shouting in relief that it was all over — or terror that it might happen again — or maybe even anger that they had been awakened so early in the morning.

Were there any exciting rescue stories?

Many, and not only about people. All kinds of things were saved, some in the strangest ways. Flags, books, money in banks, plants and flowers, and much more.

Mr. Dakin lived on Taylor Street near the top of a hill. He had been a soldier in the Civil War, and when the war was over, he began collecting American flags. By the time of the earthquake, he had a big collection.

As the fires spread into his neighborhood, soldiers told everyone to leave because it was no longer safe. But Mr. Dakin hid until everyone was gone. Then he ran his best flag up the flagpole on his roof. He lowered and raised it three times, and then left his house.

Soldiers down the hill saw the flag waving. They decided that they had to save the house from burning down. They rushed back up the hill and fought the fires for a long time. Mr. Dakin's house was the only one saved on the whole block — and all because of a waving flag!

Some of the city government's books and papers were saved in a most unexpected way. The fire engines couldn't pump water because the water pipes had broken. It seemed that all the papers would burn up.

But a quick-thinking police officer named Sergeant Behan saved some of them. He and his men rounded up some barrels of beer from nearby stores. They sprinkled the beer on the city's papers to keep them damp so that they wouldn't burn. Unfortunately, there wasn't enough beer to save everything.

Then there's the story of Alice Eastwood. She was in charge of a very famous museum of plants and flowers. As the fire came close to the museum, she climbed up and down the stairs again and again until she had saved almost all of the plants.

If Miss Eastwood had gone home, she could have saved her own things. But she didn't, and everything in her home was destroyed. She had decided that it would be easier to buy new things for her house than to find the special plants and flowers that were in the museum. The only thing of her own that she saved was the dress she was wearing.

Much of the money that was in the banks of San Francisco was saved. Charles Crocker was the head of his bank. He had bank workers put the money in large sacks. Mr. Crocker loaded the sacks onto wagons and drove down to the harbor. Then he hired a man with a boat to take all the money out into the middle of San Francisco Bay. The boat with the money stayed safely there until the fires were all out.

Were any animals saved in the nick of time?

Nearly 200 horses were rescued just when they were about to drown!

When the earthquake struck, the roof over the horse stables fell down and landed on the stall walls. The horses had to kneel or lie down — there wasn't enough room to stand up.

The stables were by the water's edge. The earthquake cracked the ground open, and water began seeping into the stalls. It rose quickly because the tide was coming in.

Then the rescue began. One person went into each stall, lifted the horse's head, and held it above the water. These men stayed in the stalls while others worked outside to break open the roof or the back walls. When big enough holes were made, the horses escaped and swam to safety. Out of 200 horses, only two were lost!

What things in your house would you try to save?

Some people had no time to pack anything. They were lucky to get out of their houses with the clothing they had on. Others had more time. They had to decide what was most important to them, since they couldn't take everything.

Almost everyone took things for sleeping. Children helped carry mattresses, sheets, blankets, and pillowcases.

Some people felt that the most important thing was to save their fancy clothes. You would see them all dressed up, walking past fallen buildings, cracked streets, and piles of broken and burned furniture.

There was no question for anyone who had a pet. Of course, you would take your pet. And so you'd see people with cats, dogs, birds in cages, bowls of goldfish, or whatever else they might have.

One woman squeezed her cat into a parrot cage, while her parrot was perched on her hand. Why do you think she did that?

Some men decided that their hats were most important to them. And so they wore all of them — one on top of the other, sometimes five high. Some people saved their jewelry. Some, their books.

Families carried frying pans, dishes, mirrors, bowls, sewing machines, lamps, rugs, chairs, and paintings. Some people even dragged their bathtubs and pianos!

And of course many children carried toys.

What do you think you would have taken?

How would you carry the things you saved?

If your family had a big trunk and suitcases, you would use them. Many people filled up pillowcases. Some rolled up as much as they could in sheets and blankets.

Today if your family moves, you would pack everything in a car or truck and drive to your new home. In 1906, very few people had cars. Some had horse-drawn wagons or carts. But most people had to carry what they were taking with them.

And that wasn't always easy. How do you think you would carry a desk, or a piano, or a bathtub?

You could tie your roller skates to the bottom and then roll it up the street. Many people did that. Families also put heavy things in baby carriages, toy wagons, or wheelbarrows. If you had a bicycle, you would strap a box to the seat and ride standing up.

Many children carried poles between them and hung bundles of clothing and other things from the pole.

One old woman was very weak and frightened. She had gotten out to the street when the quake hit. But as she looked at her house in flames, she simply couldn't move another inch. Police Officer William Desmond put *her* in a wheelbarrow and pushed her to safety!

Dragging, pulling, and pushing your goods through the broken and cracked streets was very tiring. You might have to leave a big trunk by the side of the road. With luck, it

would still be there when you came back for it.

But it seemed that the fires were following people. If you left a suitcase or chair or box behind, it probably was burned before you could go back to get it.

If people were too tired to drag their heavy trunks, they sometimes buried them. They hoped this would keep the trunks safe from the fires and from thieves.

Thieves were called "looters." Even if your house lasted through the earthquake and fires, you might still have lost everything. Looters would come in and steal all your things. Two teenage boys were caught looting. The soldiers hung signs on them. One sign said I AM A JUNK THIEF. The other said SO AM I.

Where would you live if your house was destroyed?

In the first days after the earthquake, more than half of all the people in San Francisco had to sleep outdoors. The quake and fires had ruined their homes.

Many went to the parks around the city, spread their blankets, and slept outdoors on the ground. Some people made tents. They tied ropes between poles and hung rugs, blankets, sheets, or even tablecloths over them.

Refugees (REF-you-gees) are people who leave their homes because it's not safe to stay there any longer. They find new places to live. After the earthquake and fires, the homeless people of San Francisco were called refugees. Many stayed in camps that were set up in the parks all around the city.

At first, most of the refugees lived in homemade tents. But then President Theodore Roosevelt and the United States Army Commander in Washington, D.C., ordered Army forts all around the country to ship tents and blankets to San Francisco.

The Army also built barracks for some of the refugees. These were large wooden buildings that had a number of small apartments in them.

In the fall, it became too cold and rainy to stay in tents. And there were not enough barrack apartments for everyone who had lost a home. So the city built little cottages, which were called refugee shacks. The smallest had only one room, and the biggest had three rooms. The shacks were painted green and were lined up in rows in the parks.

The city let you keep the shack if you would move it out of the camp. You had to get the shack lifted up and wheels put underneath. Then horses or mules would pull it away. By the summer of 1907, more than a year after the great earthquake, many people began to move their shacks. Everywhere you went, you saw little green houses traveling up and down the streets.

People moved their shacks to small plots of land that they bought or rented. They set the houses down and sometimes painted

them, or added porches. Some people even put two shacks together to make bigger houses. A few of these old refugee shacks are standing today, and people are still living in them.

But there was housing even more unusual than tents or barracks or shacks. Cable cars!

The earthquake had broken the cable car tracks. They had to be fixed before the cars could run again. The cable car company moved its cars to an empty lot, and the refugees moved in. Your family might have set up house in an empty cable car. The platforms in front and in back of the cars were perfect as porches.

The only problem was that as soon as the cables and tracks were fixed, you had to move out.

How would you get food and clothing?

After the earthquake, you couldn't go shopping the way you had before. Instead, you went to special centers called "relief stations" that gave out free food and clothing.

People stood in lines sometimes five blocks long to get food. They were called "bread lines" but you could get more than just bread. The centers gave out canned foods, crackers, milk, meat, vegetables, and fruit. It didn't matter whether you were rich or poor before the earthquake. Everybody stood together in the bread lines.

Other places served hot meals. You would sit down at a long table with many other people. For breakfast, you would get hash,

cereal and milk, bread, and coffee for the grown-ups. For lunch — soup and sometimes roast beef, vegetables, and bread. For supper — soup again, or a meat stew, biscuits, tea for the adults, and milk for the children.

You had to stand in line for everything. If you needed a shirt or pants, you stood in line. If you needed a skirt or blouse or dress, you stood in line. If you needed shoes or socks or a sweater or a coat, you stood in line.

In some places, you even stood in line for drinking water. The earthquake had broken the water pipes. Until they were fixed, boats brought water to San Francisco from across the bay. You would bring a bucket to the water truck and stand in line. When it was your turn, your bucket would be filled up.

What would you do if you were lost?

When the earthquake hit San Francisco, people ran into the streets. In some neighborhoods, the fires started immediately. The air was thick with smoke. Everywhere you could hear the sounds of falling beams, cracking walls, and people screaming and crying. In all the confusion, it was easy to lose sight of your family.

Families were separated in other ways, too. Your parents might tell you to stay in a certain place while they went to get help. Then, while they were gone, the soldiers would come and tell you to move because the fires were getting too close. You would have to leave before your parents came back.

There were many ways people found each other when this happened. At the camps, there were registry books. When you got there, you wrote your name in the book. Then the newspapers published the names in alphabetical order of all the people in the camps. The newspapers also listed the names of people who were missing and the names of people trying to find them.

Many people also put advertisements in newspapers. They asked their missing family members to please get in touch with them. The public libraries today still have copies of the old 1906 newspapers. A few of the advertisements that people wrote are shown on this page.

- A.B. Seal wants his mother, Sarah Seal, to call at 607 Fell Street.
- Estelle: Come to your mother on main drive of the Park.
- Byron J. Maxim, if you are living come home. Your mother is crazy. Bring May, Bessie, and boys. Mother will shelter them. Mrs. Kate Maxim.
- Harry Markowitz is looking for his mother and father. Can be found at the Denison News Co.
- Lost—Victor and Bernard Hicknan, age 10 and 7 years; dark gray suits, blue corduroy hats. Return North Beach powerhouse. Mr. Whaley.

People nailed signs on whatever was still standing on their old streets. The signs gave the new addresses where they were staying. There were also bulletin boards for notes at the camps.

Sometimes family members found each other in ways you wouldn't expect. Charles O'Day was lost for three days. On the fourth day, he went to one of the parks, climbed a tree, closed his eyes, and took a nap. His mother was in the park looking all over for him. She couldn't find him anywhere. Then she looked up, and there he was!

Many children who couldn't find their families were taken to a big tent in Golden Gate Park. One afternoon, a little dog charged under the tent ropes. He pushed his way through the crowd of children until he reached a little boy. He had found his owner and excitedly began to lick the boy's face.

But dogs were not allowed in the tent, and so a soldier threw the dog out. The little dog was not to be stopped. He rushed back into the tent and found the boy. Again the soldier threw him out. The third time that the dog ran into the tent, the soldier was going to kill him. An Army officer stopped the soldier just in time.

The officer took the little boy outside the tent and let him play with his dog. Finally, the boy and dog were both so tired they fell asleep on the grass. The boy's father had been searching for his son for days. From a distance he recognized the dog. As he got closer, he saw his son! The dog had found the boy, and the father had found the dog. At last the family was together again.

Did anyone send help to the people of San Francisco?

When they read about the earthquake in the newspapers, people from all over the country gave help to San Francisco. They sent everything you can think of: canned food, rice, blankets, mattresses, cots, shoes, shirts, pants, nightgowns, dresses, towels, tents, meat, bread, vegetables, money, candles, medicines, and even doctors and nurses.

Trainloads carrying everything arrived from Seattle, Portland, Los Angeles, Chicago, New York, Denver, and many other big cities and small towns.

Students from an Indian school in Chemewa, Oregon, baked 830 loaves of

bread and sent them to San Francisco. School children from all over the country sent their pennies and nickels to a school fund. The children's money was used to build a new school called Yerba Buena. Yerba Buena was the original Spanish name of San Francisco.

People in Japan, Mexico, Cuba, Australia, China, Russia, Belgium, France, England, Scotland, and other countries sent money to help the people of San Francisco.

Even when people couldn't send money, they gave whatever help they could. One woman wrote this letter to her friend in San Francisco:

". . . You know I have a big heart and a large house and would be only too glad to have you come and stay with me as long as you want to and it would not cost you one cent."

Were any babies born during the disaster?

Yes. When a baby is ready to be born, he or she is not about to be stopped by an earthquake or fire!

One man wrote to his relatives outside of San Francisco. He said that more than thirty babies were born in Golden Gate Park on the very day of the earthquake.

A newspaper reported that triplets were born in a tent. And every day during the week after the quake there were stories about more births.

Babies were born in the streets, in the parks, in doorways, and just about any place you can think of except hospitals. Most of the hospitals in the city were destroyed by the quake and fires.

In fact, most of the babies were born without the help of doctors or nurses. The doctors and nurses were so busy helping the sick and dying that they weren't usually around when a baby decided to come into the world.

Stories are told about babies who were given special names in honor of when and where they were born. One girl was named April Francisco Jones, and one boy was called Presidio, the name of the place in San Francisco where he was born.

Could you cook in your house after the earthquake?

Not for a long time. Even if your house was still standing and your stove looked like it could work, you were not allowed to use it.

In 1906, all stoves were connected to chimneys. And chimneys throughout San Francisco had been broken by the earthquake. You had to wait until an inspector came and said your chimney was "O.K." before you were allowed to cook in your house. The inspector didn't visit some homes for nine months.

Until they got the "O.K." from the inspector, families built stoves in the street and cooked outdoors. At first, people built small fires inside a circle of stones — the kind you might use for a campfire.

As time passed, most families built bigger stoves in the street. They might use bricks for the sides and a piece of metal on the top. Others used metal garbage cans. Before long, people built little shacks around their stoves. It was as if you were cooking in a tiny kitchen.

Children would go up and down the street checking to see what everyone else was having for dinner. You might even be given a taste of something delicious.

After the earthquake was over and the fire was out, some restaurants opened again. You would go with your family, sit down at the table, and give your order to the waiter. Then the waiter would give your order to the cook. Can you guess where? In the street, of course. Restaurants were just like houses. Until the inspector said, "O.K.," *everybody* cooked in the street.

Could you mail a letter after the earthquake?

The post office was one of the few buildings in the center of San Francisco that was still standing after the earthquake and fire. Ten brave post office workers fought off the fires day and night, and by April 20th, they were ready to send out the mail again.

There was only one problem. Almost no one had paper or envelopes or stamps. But that didn't stop anybody.

People wrote messages on the collars or cuffs of their shirts and blouses. They wrote on pieces of wood, scraps of newspaper, pages of books, and pieces of wrapping paper. So long as you had written down the correct address, the post office would send whatever you had written. You didn't even need a stamp.

The post office sent wagons out to all the refugee camps to pick up mail. The sign in front of the wagon said U.S. MAIL. People cheered when they saw the sign. It meant that at least one thing in the city was still working.

Why did it take so long to put out the fires?

The city of San Francisco was on fire for three days and nights. San Francisco is surrounded by water on three sides. Yet there was no water to put out the fires!

The earthquake shook the ground for only a minute, but it cracked the gas pipes and split electric wires. Sparks from wood and coal fires and the electric wires burst into raging flames when they hit the escaping gas.

The quake also broke all the fire alarms. Fire fighters knew where to go only when they saw flames and smoke. By the time they arrived, it was often too late. Many fires burned without anyone there to stop them.

Even when the fire engines arrived on time, there was trouble. Little or no water came out of the fire hoses because the hydrants were empty — the earthquake had broken most of the water pipes.

Fire Chief Dennis Sullivan was badly hurt during the earthquake and died a few days later. It was hard to figure out what to do when the leader of all the fire fighters was dead. Different people began giving orders, sometimes an Army general, or the police chief, or the mayor, or the new fire chief. And sometimes these people disagreed with each other about the best thing to do.

One way to fight fires is to use dynamite. Let's say the fire is coming near a street where there are many wooden houses that

will burn quickly. All the houses on the block might catch fire because the sparks often leap over from one building to the next.

And so you use dynamite to blow up some of the houses. When they fall down, there won't be anything for the sparks to jump to. The fire will have no place to go and it will die out.

But you have to be very careful when you use dynamite to fight fires. You have to watch the wind and know just how far the sparks will fly.

Most people didn't know how to use it. Instead of stopping fires, they started more. Many houses in San Francisco were made of wood, so there was plenty of fuel to feed the fires.

Finally, with help from the Navy and the Marines, the fire fighters got long hoses and pumped water from San Francisco Bay. Then at last luck came to San Francisco — the wind changed direction. Instead of blowing over the land and spreading the fires, it blew out to sea. After three long days, the fires were out at last.

How did people keep their spirits up?

It wasn't easy after an earthquake that shook up your world, and then fires that burned down your city. But the people of San Francisco did many things to cheer themselves up.

If a family had saved their piano from the flames, at night everyone would gather in the street and sing. The music drowned out the sounds of the crackling fires, the falling walls, and the dynamiting.

People also tried to keep their sense of humor. Sometimes they cracked jokes as they walked through the streets carrying their bundles. One man put down the heavy suitcase he was carrying, sat on it, and began to play his banjo. From where he sat, he could see the fires burning all over the city. When he began to sing, he picked the perfect song. It was called "There'll Be a Hot Time in the Old Town Tonight!"

People told jokes about the tents they lived in, the food they ate, and anything else you might think of.

The outdoor kitchens were a favorite place to put up signs.

One sign on a street kitchen said:

MAKE THE BEST OF IT —

FORGET THE REST OF IT.

Many people put signs on their tents. They said silly things, such as:

RING THE BELL FOR LANDLADY, or

ROOMS FOR RENT, or

ALL SHOOK UP!

When the quake was over and the fires were out, people began to rebuild the city. And they kept on putting up signs. On the wall of one new building were the words:

FIRST TO SHAKE

FIRST TO BURN

FIRST TO TAKE

ANOTHER NEW TURN!

59

How long did it take San Francisco to recover?

Some things were fixed quickly, some took more time. What would you have fixed first? This is the way it happened in San Francisco.

The post office was delivering and sending out mail in less than five days after the earthquake.

There were a few grocery stores, meat markets, and restaurants that were back in business within a week.

It took more than ten days to get the water running properly. And lights were back working on the main streets in less than two weeks. But lights in your house might have taken months to come back on because so many of the electric wires had been destroyed.

Many of the trolley cars and cable cars were running again within two weeks. The biggest problem was clearing the streets of all the rubble from the broken and burned buildings.

It took months to get all the chimneys inspected. Until then, you had to cook in the street. It also took months to get the fire alarm system working. This might have caused a serious problem, but it didn't. People were very careful about lighting fires after the terrible days of fire.

All the schools closed down right after the earthquake. Many had been destroyed. Others were used as relief stations to give out supplies to people. One was even used as police headquarters because the real police station had burned down.

During May and June, some classes were held in tents in the parks. But it wasn't like school, and not many students could attend. Most students didn't go back until the end of September.

Many small stores lost everything during the earthquake and fire. A special committee was set up by the city government to help these stores get started again. The committee gave money to grocers, bricklayers, carpenters, barbers, tailors, boatmakers, printers, shoemakers, and a cigarmaker.

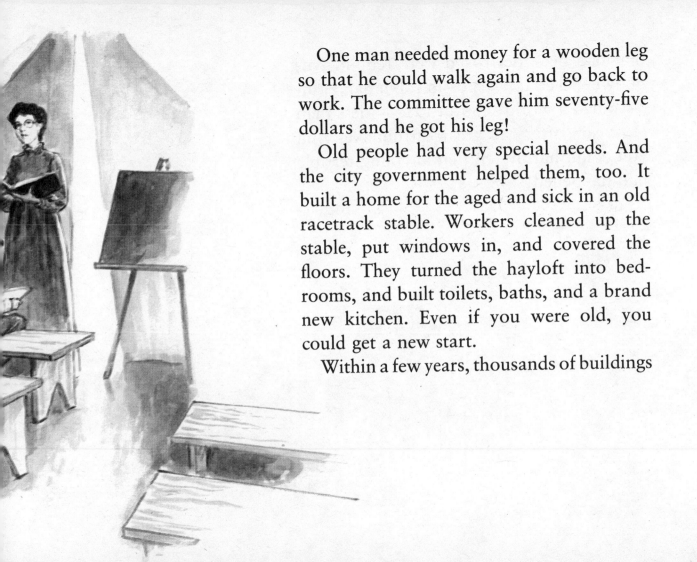

One man needed money for a wooden leg so that he could walk again and go back to work. The committee gave him seventy-five dollars and he got his leg!

Old people had very special needs. And the city government helped them, too. It built a home for the aged and sick in an old racetrack stable. Workers cleaned up the stable, put windows in, and covered the floors. They turned the hayloft into bedrooms, and built toilets, baths, and a brand new kitchen. Even if you were old, you could get a new start.

Within a few years, thousands of buildings

that had been destroyed were rebuilt. No-body believed it was possible, but San Francisco had a world's fair in 1915 — less than ten years after the great earthquake. And you could hardly tell that anything terrible had happened!